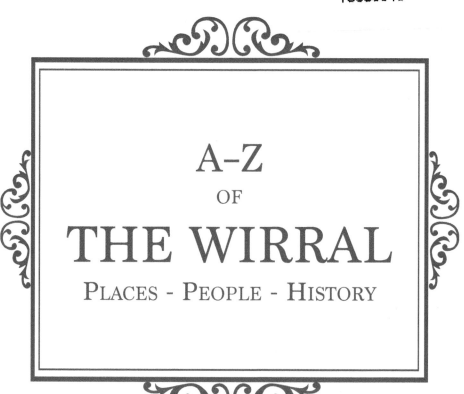

A–Z
OF
THE WIRRAL
PLACES - PEOPLE - HISTORY

Les Jones

AMBERLEY

For Deb and for George

First published 2022

Amberley Publishing
The Hill, Stroud, Gloucestershire, GL5 4EP
www.amberley-books.com

Copyright © Les Jones, 2022

The right of Les Jones to be identified as the
Author of this work has been asserted in
accordance with the Copyrights, Designs and
Patents Act 1988.

ISBN 978 1 3981 0936 0 (print)
ISBN 978 1 3981 0937 7 (ebook)

British Library Cataloguing in Publication Data.
A catalogue record for this book is available
from the British Library.

Typesetting by SJmagic DESIGN SERVICES,
India. Printed in Great Britain.

Contents

Introduction

The Wirral Peninsula is one of the most disparate regions in the country. Separated by two exceptionally diverse rivers, Wirral boasts sandy beaches, wind-swept views across to Wales, bustling towns and quiet country lanes. Its people are equally diverse, with many national and international personalities hailing from the peninsula. This A–Z is a personal choice, a snapshot of Wirral as it was and is. I hope you will enjoy meeting Beefy and Boatie; Tom, Dick and Harry; the quarrymen and the Beatles; kings and queens; and the man who was chased by a group of irate lamas. Learn about the man who frightened off Napoleon and his cohorts with a pair of wooden guns, discover the location of a State secret where unidentified flying objects are on show, marvel at the greatest array of Pre-Raphaelites in the UK and take a look around the village made from soap. Read about a 75-foot-high wedding cake, a borstal that floated, a boat that hovered and a house that moved 3 miles down the road. We have famous sports personalities, comedians, mountaineers and actors, peers and poets. And for those luminaries who due to lack of space have missed the cut, I can only apologise – such is the lexicon of life.

Argyle Theatre

Also known as the Argyle Theatre of Varieties and rather more grandly as the Prince of Wales Theatre, The Argyle opened its doors in 1868 with a full bill of entertainment, which included the Cedas Troupe of Minstrels; the Hondras Brothers, who were classical gymnasts; the snappily titled Fothergill and Summerson, Irish comedians; and, rather bizarrely, M. Bevani and his wooden-headed family, presumably a forerunner of the ever-popular Woodentops.

It was one of the grandest theatres in Wirral, with seating for 800 patrons, several bars and a 70-foot-long bowling alley for good measure. The justification for the popularity and longevity of the Argyle is apparent from the notable list of nationally known entertainers that once walked the boards here. Dan Leno, Georges

The Argyle Theatre in the 1930s.

Robey and Formby, Vesta Tilley, Harry Lauder, Bud Flanagan and Chesney Allen all appeared here. Charlie Chaplin, a comic genius apparently, played here back in the day, but never on the same bill as the genuinely hilarious Stan Laurel, who had the audiences rocking with laughter well before he teamed up with Oliver Hardy. Morecambe and Wise also played the Argyle, indeed the theatre was mentioned in one of the pair's most famous sketches when they invited Andre Preview onto their Christmas special in 1971. All this frivolity came to an end in September 1940 when the German Luftwaffe arrived uninvited and gutted the building with a high-explosive bomb. The site was cleared in 1972 and is now a car park for a department store.

Atherton, James

The founder of New Brighton. After an accomplished career as a grocer, Atherton had amassed enough money to pronounce himself a merchant and latterly a gentleman. Despite his undoubted success in the grocery trade, he nevertheless felt the need to try his hand at property speculation and to this end bought a large tract of land in Everton. This venture proved immensely profitable, so much so that he felt able to donate some of his land for the building of St George's Church. From this elevated position above the city, he must have gazed over to the windswept sand dunes of north Wirral and wondered if he could have equal success on the other side of the river.

New Brighton from the beach in 1903.

Joined by his son-in-law William Rowson, he bought a sizable tract of dunes from the lord of the manor, John Penkett, and set about erecting a number of grand mansions on the steeply sloping land, each with its own panoramic view of the Mersey. Two of the best sites were taken by Atherton and Rowson at the end of Wellington Road, which at that time sloped down directly onto the beach. Neither house survives. Sadly, Atherton did not live to see the fruits of his labours, dying in 1838. He may not have been enamoured with the subsequent fate of the resort, which moved rapidly from select gentleman's retreat to brassy seaside resort in a few short years.

New Brighton from the air in 1921.

B

Battle of Brunanburgh

The site of this important but little-known battle has been fought over by academics for many years. The renowned medievalist Michael Wood is convinced that the battle site is located near a lay-by in Doncaster, but the good professor may be getting confused, as every Wirralian knows that the Battle of Brunanburgh took place in Bromborough in AD 937, marked on old Ordnance Survey maps as 'Wargraves, supposed site of battle between Aethelstan and the Danes' and situated where Commercial Road now stands. Its huge significance lies in the fact that it established the boundaries of England, Scotland and Wales, the borders of which are largely the ones we recognise today. Before Brunanburgh Britain was divided up between several kings and earls, all vying for land and power. Celts in the far north, the Norse earls in the north of England, Owein in Wales and the Anglo-Saxons in central and southern England.

The Anglo-Saxon King Athelstan, grandson of Alfred the Great, took on the Celts and Norse army that had ravaged the land as far south as Bromborough – the battle sounded like quite a brouhaha. The *Anglo-Saxon Chronicle* stated that 'no slaughter yet was greater made e'er in this island, of people slain, before this time, with the edge of the sword'. After the battle Athelstan was able to unite Wessex and Mercia to create England.

Beatles, The

A popular beat combo from the 1960s who appeared many times at various venues on Wirral. Their first appearance was at the Grosvenor Ballroom in Wallasey, where they were to play on no fewer than fourteen occasions, a record only beaten by the Tower Ballroom in New Brighton, which hosted the Fab Four twenty-seven times. Wirral can boast the first official Beatles fan club, the first publicity photo shots, the first appearance of Ringo, the first time they wore suits (made in Birkenhead, incidentally) and their first radio broadcast. Other gigs were held at such diverse places as Neston Institute, Irby Hall and the Apollo Roller Rink in Moreton.

Most of the band had personal connections to Wirral, Paul McCartney having several cousins in Bebington (Kate and Ted Robbins et al.). The most heart-breaking connection was perhaps that of John Lennon, whose Auntie Annie lived in a house called Ardmore in Old Chester Road, where John spent many happy times in his younger days. He talked fondly of having a family reunion there in 1980, a wish that was cruelly dashed when his life was cut short by a sad fantasist. With added poignancy, the only photograph known to exist of John with his mother Julia was taken here in the front garden in 1948, ten years before her equally untimely death in a road accident. 'Her hair of floating sky is shimmering, glimmering in the sun.' ('Julia', *The Beatles* aka 'The White Album', 1968)

Bidston Court

This was one of the grandest mansions in Wirral, originally constructed on Bidston Ridge in the late Victorian era, built at a cost of £150,000 for the soap manufacturer Robert William Hudson in 1891. The famous architectural historian Nikolaus Pevsner thought it 'one of the most notable essays in half-timbered design anywhere in the country'. It was designed in an Elizabethan style by the architectural firm of Grayson and Oulds, who were responsible for many prominent buildings in Wirral, notably Hamilton Square station and work for Lord Leverhulme in Thornton Hough and Port Sunlight, including the Lever Club, the school and the Bridge Inn.

The mansion was eventually acquired through his mother-in-law by Sir Ernest Royden, a wealthy shipowner who fell in love with the place. The views from the south at the time stretched across the Fender Valley, with distant aspects of the North Wales coast. With remarkable prescience, however, Royden foresaw the deterioration of this fine vista, which is now scarred by tower blocks and the incessant rumble of the M53. But what to do about it? Most people would just move to a better location, but Sir Ernest came up with a rather more radical solution: he moved the house.

Between 1928 and 1931 the entire mansion was moved to Frankby, 3 miles to the west. Incredibly there is footage of this remarkable undertaking available on YouTube – very grainy and only a minute long, it is a remarkable slice of history none the less. Each stone block and baulk of timber was carefully prised apart and numbered before being transported to the sylvan setting of Royden Park where the whole mansion was reconstructed and renamed Hill Bark where it stands to this day, now functioning as a hotel.

The only evidence left on the original site is a small, terraced area called Bidston Court Gardens, now owned by the council, hidden behind an anonymous rock-faced wall in Vyner Road South, and the original lodge, a Grade II listed building in its own right with fine pargetted panels on both floors, also created by Grayson and Ould.

A busy scene at Bidston Court in 1897.

Bidston Court in its new location in Royden Park.

Birdspotting

The Wirral Peninsula is blessed with some of the best birdwatching opportunities in the world. It is such an important area that the Royal Society for the Protection of Birds has set up a large viewing and information facility at Burton Mere Wetlands Reserve to the west of the peninsula overlooking the freshwater wetlands of the Dee. All along the western and northern coasts there are excellent viewpoints from which to observe large flocks of waders and geese, and rarer seasonal visitors to our shores.

West Kirby and Hilbre Island are perfect spots for viewing birds, but the following list of sightings for a short period in February 2021 provides a good idea of the variety of places where rare species can be seen: a water pipit on Neston Marsh, a green sandpiper on flooded fields by Benty Heath Lane in Willaston, goosanders and brent geese at West Kirby Marine Lake, a red kite at Arrowbrook, a hen harrier at Parkgate, a peregrine falcon at Denhall Quay and even a firecrest at Heswall. There were also more sightings of black-tailed godwits than you could shake a stick at. All this activity is here in abundance for those with eyes to see (and a good pair of binoculars).

Birkenhead Park

One of the best public parks in the United Kingdom, Birkenhead Park is also one of the most historic, being the very first publicly funded civic park in the world. It was the brainchild of Sir William Jackson, Liverpool merchant and philanthropist who felt that the ever-expanding population of Birkenhead would need a place of recreation among the rapidly rising tide of housing. Designed by no less a figure than Sir Joseph Paxton, architect of the Crystal Palace and head gardener at the Duke of Cavendish's Chatsworth estate. Paxton created lakes within the estate, using the spoil to create the surrounding hills and rockery. Several structures were created to enhance the view, notably the fine bandstand and the Swiss bridge, and wonderful lodges located at every entrance, each reflecting different architectural styles – Italianate, Norman, Gothic, castellated – and of course the grand entrance in Park Road North, designed by Lewis Hornblower in an Ionic idiom, which is now listed Grade II*.

Opened on Easter Monday 1847 by Lord Morpeth, on the same day as the newly created dock system, the whole town seemed to have turned up for the event. Festivities included sack races, greasy pole climbing and the chasing of a shaved pig with a greased tail – simple pleasures. Many nationally important events have taken place in the park, one of the few to have an extant memorial to it is the Welsh Eisteddfod of 1917, an itinerant event usually held in Wales but in this instance moved to Birkenhead as there were so many Welshmen working in the town at the time. The memorial is located at Cannon Hill in the lower park. The park was listed as a Grade I landscape by English Heritage in 1995 and after a period of neglect was tastefully renovated following a lottery fund grant of £11.5 million in 2007.

The main entrance to Birkenhead Park.

The old bandstand at Birkenhead Park.

Birkenhead Priory

Monastic life was a major facet of religious and secular life in England since St Augustine's efforts to re-establish Christianity in AD 597. Many of the 700 or so monastic buildings and religious communities were destroyed, however, during Henry VIII's purges, ranging from tiny establishments with a handful of brethren to large groups with several hundred members. Birkenhead Priory fell into the former category, with just sixteen monks when it was founded by Hamon de Massey of Dunham Massey in Cheshire. It claimed rights of fishing and retrieving wreckage in the Mersey, and owned a surprising amount of land in Wirral, its grange being located at the end of what is now Grange Road in Birkenhead.

After the dissolution, the estate passed to Ralph Worsley of Lancashire, who let the buildings become ruinous, with only the chapter house surviving intact. This is still a place of worship, now owned by the Church of England. St Mary's Church was built in 1821 by Thomas Rickman in the grounds of the priory to cater for the expanding urban population but has subsequently been partly demolished after closure in 1974 due to safety reasons, apart from the tower and two flanking walls. The priory has also lost most of its churchyard to the expanded shipyard to the east, but the burial vault of the Laird family remains. The priory became a Grade I listed building in 1979 and the whole site is a Scheduled Ancient Monument, although it is perhaps underappreciated due to its location, hemmed in by shipyards to the east and a flyover to the west.

Inside the chapel at Birkenhead Priory.

The chapter house and scriptorium at Birkenhead Priory.

Birkenhead Rules

As the ship starts to slowly sink at the port bow, the cry goes up: 'Abandon ship, take to the lifeboats', followed by 'Women and children first'. This laudable conduct came to be known as the Birkenhead Rules or the Birkenhead Drill, although it has no actual basis in maritime law. This protocol was named after a famous incident in 1852 when the troopship HMS *Birkenhead* hit submerged rocks and began to sink. The captain ordered his men to line up on the deck and assist all the women and children into the limited number of lifeboats. This particular action gained wide attention through a depiction of the events in a famous painting by Thomas Hemy called *The Wreck of the Birkenhead*, painted in 1892. It is, however, better known through its association with the sinking of RMS *Titanic* in 1912. In an awful twist of fate, Captain Smith's orders for women and children first was interpreted in different ways by his officers: some thought the orders were for women and children only to be allowed in the boats, causing boats to be launched half empty, while other officers filled the half-empty boats with men if no women or children could be found to fill the places. This led to over 80 per cent of women and children surviving the sinking while less than half that number of men survived. All this altruism would have been unnecessary if ships had simply been provided with enough lifeboats. The reason often given by ship owners was that additional boats would encumber the decks; the more likely reason would no doubt have been cost.

The Birkenhead depicted on the side of a Woodside pub.

Boode, Margaret

For centuries, the northern and eastern shores of the Wirral Peninsula had been feared by mariners when the stormy waters of Liverpool Bay were at their worst. In addition to the clear dangers of shipwreck and drowning was the extra dread of the infamous wreckers who lay in wait to take advantage of some unfortunate half-drowned sailor who had managed to drag himself ashore. Few people dared to interfere with this nefarious activity, but one outstanding lady who took pity on these seafarers in their hour of greatest need was Lady Margaret Boode of Leasowe Castle.

Known as the 'Samaritans of the Cheshire Coast', Mrs Boode and her staff would rescue sailors from the beaches and remove them to the safely and warmth of the castle where they were fed and cared for until they regained their strength. Mrs Boode was married to Lewis W. Boode, a West Indian planter (for 'planter' read slave owner), but was also the daughter of the Rector of Liverpool, so was in a morally uncomfortable position. Whether this fuelled her altruism is not known, but her numerous acts of kindness were to save many lives. Sadly, she died in a fall from her pony carriage in 1826, an event that was immortalised by her grieving daughter in a memorial that still exists today. Moved from its original position opposite Darley Dene in Breck Road in Wallasey due to bomb damage in the Second World War, it can be found among the undergrowth near the bridge across the motorway approach road.

The Boode Memorial on Breck Road in 1910.

The Boode Memorial today.

Botham, Ian

It was a gloriously hot day in the summer of 1981. The third Ashes test was not going well, however. After scoring 401-9 the Australians decided to declare their innings and force England to follow on; they needed 227 runs just to avoid an innings defeat. The home side's chances appeared rather bleak. Then up stepped Beefy Botham. Ably assisted by Graham Dilley, Chris Old and Bob Willis with partnerships of 117, 67 and 37, respectively, for the 8th, 9th and 10th wickets, he began smashing the Aussies out of the park. A couple of boundaries through mid-wicket, a hefty blow down to cow corner, peerless drives straight down the ground, twenty-seven fours and a six brought Botham 149 and the Australians now had to bat again. Needing a paltry 130 to win, they reached 50 for the loss of one wicket. Bob Willis then changed ends and proceeded to take 8 for 43. The Aussies were all out for 111 – Nelson would have been proud (cricketers will get this reference). It was only the second time in cricketing history that a side had won a match after being asked to follow on.

Born in Heswall in 1955, Ian Botham was one of those larger-than-life characters Britain seems to produce in abundance. He has done stalwart work for children's leukaemia charities in between his sporting career, which brought him a well-deserved OBE, and has done much tv work, as a captain on *A Question of Sport* and later as a cricketing commentator. He received a knighthood in 2007 and would later be elevated to the House of Lords as Baron Botham.

Cammell Lairds

The origins of Cammell Laird shipbuilders began not on the Mersey but along a small tidal creek running west of the river at Wallasey Pool where, in 1824, William Laird set up an ironworks to construct boilers. He was joined by his son John in 1828 when they began to construct vessels on a small scale, the HMS *Birkenhead* being the most well known (see Birkenhead Rules). In 1857 they moved to the Mersey shore where the extra space enabled them to build larger ships, such as the infamous CCS *Alabama*, which was commissioned by the Confederates during the American Civil War and wrought such havoc that the British government ended up paying the US government compensation of £3.25 million.

Cammell Lairds viewed from the priory tower.

In 1903 Lairds merged with Sheffield steel producers Charles Cammell & Co. and increased capacity at the yard, which enabled them to be in an excellent position to supply the navy at the outbreak of the First World War with five light cruisers, six destroyers, two escorts and eight submarines. This figure was dwarfed, however, during the Second World War when nine battleships, eleven aircraft carriers and over 200 other fighting ships were produced or repaired at the yard, a massive contribution to the war effort. The famous *Ark Royal* had been completed just before the outbreak of war, along with the *Mauritania*, which, while not a fighting ship, proved invaluable as a troop carrier as she was the largest ship ever built in an English shipyard.

After the war Cammell Lairds fell on hard times and were nationalised in 1977. They have since been de-nationalised, closed, leased out and partially reopened. They have recently secured a contract to produce Dreadnought submarines and built and fitted out the Antarctic exploration vessel *Boaty McBoatface*.

Craig, Daniel

Although born in Chester, Daniel Craig moved to Hoylake at an early age and soon became involved in acting, becoming interested in school plays from the age of six. He moved to Hilbre High School in West Kirby, but it was when he moved up to Calday Grange Grammar School that he was spotted while accompanying a friend to an audition of the school play. Although he was not there to audition, a music teacher noticed him and thought that he had the perfect face to play an undertaker, so he got the part of Mr Sowerberry in the school's adaptation of Charles Dickens' *Oliver Twist*. Having been bitten by the acting bug, he went on to train at the National Youth Theatre.

After smaller parts on TV in *Heartbeat, Drop the Dead Donkey* and *Between the Lines*, he landed a major role as Geordie Peacock in the hit series *Our Friends in the North*, which is generally regarded as his breakthrough role. Film roles followed, with appearances in such films as *Road to Perdition, Layer Cake* and *Lara Croft: Tomb Raider* before becoming the sixth James Bond in *Casino Royale* in 2006. He brought a vitality to the role that the franchise had started to lose and went on to appear as Bond in *Quantum of Solace* in 2008 and *Skyfall* in 2012. The latest Bond film, *No Time to Die*, was released in autumn 2021. It appears that this may be his last outing as the suave, hell-raising spy, only time will tell.

Dawpool

Overlooking the River Dee with the dark Clwydian hills beyond, Dawpool presented a brooding presence high on the treeless Thurstaston headland. It was built for Thomas Ismay of the White Star Shipping Line by one of the most productive and influential Gothic architects of the nineteenth century, Richard Norman Shaw. Despite costing a fortune to create, it was never popular with the Ismay family and has been described by Andrew Saint, Shaw's biographer, as 'lowering in shadow in rainfall, bleached in sunlight, in accord with the rich yet baleful red of the Wirral sandstone from which it is fashioned'. It did, however, incorporate many of the innovations designed for Shaw's

Richard Norman Shaw's Dawpool in 1890.

more famous mansion of Cragside in Northumberland, built for the millionaire arms manufacturer Sir William Armstrong. An underground railway in the basement for coal transportation gives some idea of the scale of this huge edifice.

One lasting thing Thomas Ismay did at Dawpool can be witnessed by anyone driving past the Cottage Loaf at Thurstaston towards West Kirby. He felt that the existing road was too close to his mansion, so he brought in dozens of workers to dig a deep cutting through the sandstone and moved the road away from his mansion. How the other half live, eh?

The Ismay family sold the property soon after Thomas' death and after a short spell as an officers' orthopaedic hospital during the First World War it was sold on and scandalously demolished in 1927 as it was 'surplus to requirements'. Such was the quality of the construction that it took copious amounts of dynamite to bring it down. Remnants of this fine building survive, however, most noticeably one of the enormous mantelpieces, which eccentric architect Clough Williams Ellis bought and reused in Portmeirion, a flight of fancy he created in North Wales, using it as the frontispiece for his Pantheon building. Another fireplace was removed and placed in the foyer of the Kingsland restaurant in Borough Road, Birkenhead.

Dixie Dean

William Ralph 'Dixie' Dean was born at No. 313 Laird Street, Birkenhead, on 22 January 1907. Do not seek his shrine, however, as the site is now a petrol station next to a KFC. Like many people he loved football, but Dixie was keener than most. He attended the nearby Albert Memorial Industrial School because the footballing facilities were better than at other schools. When he left school and got a job as a fitter with the Wirral Railway, he volunteered for the unpopular night shifts so that he could practice his footballing skills during the day.

It was when he was playing for Pensby FC that he was spotted by a sharp-eyed Tranmere Rovers scout and promptly signed up, staying with Rovers for sixteen months, where he made thirty appearances, scoring twenty-seven goals. With these sort of stats it was not long before the big boys took an interest. Arsenal and Newcastle United both expressed a desire to sign Dixie, but it was the team he had supported as a boy that he eventually signed for, leaving Tranmere Rovers for Everton in March 1925 for a then record fee of £3,000.

This fairy tale progress all came to a crashing halt, however, when he was involved in a serious motorcycle accident in North Wales and suffered a fractured skull and broken jaw. Despite predictions to the contrary, he returned to football in the 1927–28 campaign when he scored the never-to-be beaten 60 goals in a single season, helping Everton to the First Division title, an achievement they were to repeat in 1932, along with the FA Cup in 1933. He was capped for the first time for England in 1927, scoring 18 goals in his sixteen appearances.

The Second World War ended his playing career and he ended up running The Dublin Packet pub in Chester for many years. He died while attending an Everton vs Liverpool match in 1980 at the age of seventy-three. A fitting tribute was paid to him when he was one of just twenty-two players inducted into the inaugural English Football Hall of Fame.

Docklands

The docks at Birkenhead and Wallasey, known collectively as the Great Float, were the transport hub for most of the trade in and out of Wirral in the nineteenth century. Created originally as a rival to the mighty docks on the Liverpool side of the Mersey, they were never a total success and were soon incorporated into the Mersey Docks and Harbour Board. The first docks created were on the Birkenhead side, near to Woodside Ferry. Morpeth and Egerton Docks were opened in 1847, on the same day as Birkenhead Park. Morpeth Dock, named after Lord Morpeth, 7th Earl of Carlisle, provided berths for ships of the Bibby and Brocklebank Lines, with a branch dock to

The old accumulator tower at Birkenhead Docks.

the south-east, which was operated as a goods station for the GWR. This was later filled in to provide room for the monolithic brick ventilation shaft for the Queensway Tunnel. Egerton Dock was used by the LNWR for the same purpose.

Wallasey Dock was constructed to the north to provide grain storage and later for imported livestock. It was only accessed from the East Float and was eventually filled in to make room for the Stena Ferry Terminal. The northernmost dock is Alfred Dock, named after Prince Alfred, the second son of Queen Victoria, who opened the dock in 1866. This is now the only dock providing access to the river. The large tower to the west of the dock provided hydraulic power for the bascule bridges and cranes on the dock estate. The only other major dock was the Vittoria, opened in 1909 and named after the Peninsular War battle of 1813. It was used by the Clan Line Steamers operating in the Far East and was home for a while to the training ship HMS *Conway*. The north side of the float here housed the largest milling warehouses in the world at one time. Most have gone, but the remaining rather sombre-looking block has been converted into flats.

Moving west again, Duke Street bridge leads to the West Float, which housed graving docks and warehousing. There was a further dock beyond the Penny Bridge known as Bidston Dock, but this was short-lived and was used initially to lay up vessels before being turned into an iron ore terminal with three giant cranes and a substantial rail system that transferred ore from ship to train and on to nearby Shotton Steel Works. The dock closed in 2000 and was subsequently filled in.

Grain warehouse on the East Float.

Ellesmere Port Boat Museum

The existence of Ellesmere Port can be found in the iron foundries of Shropshire. Correctly regarded as the cradle of the Industrial Revolution, the area around Ironbridge became the hub of the iron-making industry. Within the space of a few years the demand for iron for the overseas market reinforced the need to find an efficient means to get iron out of the gorge and into large ports such as Bristol and Liverpool. The solution lay in the Shropshire Union Canal, which ran from Ellesmere in Shropshire to Netherpool on the banks of the Mersey, where goods were transhipped on to seagoing vessels. The eastern end of the canal became known as Ellesmere Port and was rapidly built up with warehouses and other vital infrastructure, much of it designed by Thomas Telford. What remained in the area after fires and demolition formed the basis for the Boat Museum, including the remaining Telford buildings, a row of dockers' cottages called Porters Row, a small lighthouse and a pump house from 1874.

The Manchester Ship Canal beside the museum.

The stars of the show, however, are the floating exhibits: some thirty-five barges of various sizes and ages, bought with grants or on permanent loan. The museum was formed to preserve these barges so as not to lose a vital link in the countries' commercial heritage. The whole dock area was cleared of the detritus of years of neglect by a stalwart army of volunteers who gladly gave up their free time for the common good. Opened in 1976, the National Waterways Museum, which is its current incarnation, remains primarily a living museum and a visit is thoroughly recommended.

Fort Perch Rock

Once the enormous tower at New Brighton had been dismantled after the First World War, the greatest landmark remaining was Fort Perch Rock, standing solid and four square on the Black Rock, a few hundred feet away from the promenade. Despite this prominent position, however, the existence of the fort was an official secret until the 1930s and did not appear on any contemporary Ordnance Survey maps, a cunning plan re-employed by the Ministry of Defence in the 1960s when the Post Office Tower in London was also left off OS maps, this time to outwit the KGB. Completed on 30 April 1829, the fort was built to protect the Rock Channel and the seaward approaches to Liverpool from marauding Gallic warships at a time when the British were regularly at war with the dastardly French. There had been talk of placing guns on the lighthouse or a light on the fort but neither of these fanciful schemes came to pass.

Fort Perch Rock from New Brighton Promenade.

Fort Perch Rock from the sands.

Designed by Captain John Kitson of the Royal Engineers, it had sufficient accommodation for over a hundred officers and men. It even came with its own well for the supply of fresh water in the unlikely event of it being besieged by the French. It housed eighteen guns, nearly all large 32 pounders, which were the largest available at the time. It fired its guns in anger just twice – at the beginning of the First and Second World Wars. It was eventually decommissioned in 1956 and in more peaceful times it became a museum housing bits and pieces from downed aircraft.

Francis, Thomas

Wirral's most famous home-grown eccentric. Francis was a stone mason by trade and he utilised his skills to create the most bizarre and fascinating artifacts. Unfortunately, most of his work has been lost over the years, but what remains is intriguing enough. Set into a low wall just inside Mayer Park in Bebington are the puzzle stones, now his only surviving work. They comprise a set of riddles carved into the stone. One example should suffice:

From six take nine	S I X	= S
From nine take ten	I X	= I
From forty take fifty	X L	= X
Then six will remain		

It's all down to Roman numerals.

Not content with beguiling the locals, he covered his nearby house with sculpture of every description and installed a couple of wooden cannons on the roof to deter Napoleon and his Gallic hordes if they were so impertinent as to rock up in the village. He also dug and lined his own grave and took great delight in brushing it out each Saturday and lying in it smoking his pipe. Despite this somewhat morbid behaviour he lived to a ripe old age. I will leave it to Nathaniel Hawthorne, American Consul to Liverpool at the time, to express what most people must have thought of Mr Francis:

> In the village of Bebington we saw a house built in imitation of a castle, with turrets in which an upper and under row of cannons were mounted. On the wall there were eccentric inscriptions cut into slabs of stone, but I could make no sense of these. We peeped through the gate and saw a piazza beneath which seemed to stand the figure of a man. He appeared advanced in years, and was dressed in a blue coat and buff breaches, with a straw hat on his head. Behold too, a dog sitting chained. Also close behind the gateway, was another man seated. All were images, and the dwelling with the inscriptions and queer statuary was probably the whim of some half-crazed person.

The Rubbing Stones in Mayer Park.

G

Great Eastern, The

The early history of this great ship is not a local one; however, what became of it is where the Wirral connection comes in. Isambard Kingdom Brunel's famous iron steamship was constructed on the Thames near Millwall and spent most of its life laying cables under the Atlantic Ocean. When she had outgrown her usefulness, she was bought by the owners of Lewis's department store in Liverpool as a floating advertisement, steaming miserably up and down the Mersey, like a once proud lion pacing up and down in its cage, a sad and ignominious end for a magnificent and pioneering vessel. Bizarrely the advertising on the side of the ship had the legend 'Lewis's are the friends of the people'. What on God's earth did that mean? Having done with mocking Brunel's masterpiece, the poor ship was eventually sold for scrap, fetching £16,000 at auction. It was beached off the east Wirral coast at New Ferry foreshore in 1889 and it took a full eighteen months to be taken apart, with bits and

New Ferry foreshore, final resting place of the *Great Eastern*.

pieces finding their way to the nearby eponymously named pub. The top mast was sold to Everton Football Club as a flagpole.

There were gruesome stories at the time of the dismantlers finding two skeletons in the cavity of the double hull, the remains of a welder and his boy who were accidentally sealed up within the hull during construction. Alas, this interesting story, like most such bone-chilling tales, is completely untrue. Inspection hatches were inserted in the hull so that such an occurrence could not happen, and the voids were regularly inspected and cleaned during the life of the ship, at which time any remains would have been discovered. Remains of the actual ship, however, were discovered by Tony Robinson and the *Time Team* gang during an episode about the Great Eastern. Geophys found evidence to suggest residual parts from the keel still remain on the foreshore.

H

Half Man Half Biscuit

The band may have formed just for a laugh and their name might be the oddest since the Bonzo's, and their lyrics are often witty and hilarious, but these are seriously good musicians. They were formed in 1984 by Nigel Blackwell and Neil Crossley and soon to be joined by two members of punky pub band Attempted Moustache. Despite changes in line-ups, they are still performing to this day, having the longevity of one of Peter Kay's well-dunked hobnobs.

Their debut album *Back in the DHSS* went to Number One in the indie charts, with their second offering reaching Number Two. What also appeals to fans, however, is their seeming disinterest in the trappings of success, famously turning down an appearance on Channel Four's *The Tube* because it clashed with a Tranmere Rovers match, even though they had been offered the use of a helicopter to get them to the match after the gig.

HMHB drummer Carl Henry – the early years.

During their Voyage to the Bottom of the Road they have produced fourteen fine albums, and who can say they have never sung along to their indie chart hits 'The Trumpton Riots' and 'Joy Division Oven Glove'? These four lads who shook the Wirral may never get a statue like the Fab Four, but, judging by the standard of Beatles statuary, would they want one?

Hamilton Square

Birkenhead in the early nineteenth century was something of a boom town. From a sleepy backwater on the eastern coast of Wirral in 1810 with an ancient priory, a few sheep and nothing much else, its position opposite the expanding conurbation of

The Town Hall at Hamilton Square.

Hamilton Square looking east.

Liverpool meant it was prime real estate for industrial and commercial entrepreneurs to take advantage of. The pioneers of this expansion had grandiose plans for the town, with a beautiful set-piece square to equal those being created in London, fed by long, straight roads leading off into the distance, lined with large mansions for the new middle-class merchants. It is of great regret that these grand plans were not fully realised. Hamilton Square was built with a few nearby streets in a similar vein, along with a few outliers such as the Queens Hotel and the Angel Inn, but the long streets never received their grand villas, being built up eventually with small artisans' houses. What was created, however, was a grand square of Georgian buildings, built in rows of which no two are the same, all now listed as Grade I, the largest concentration of such buildings outside London.

William Laird had commissioned the Edinburgh architect Gillespie Graham to erect the square in a similar manner to his Scottish designs, with a central garden for the exclusive use of the owners. A space was left for the town hall, which was only completed some fifty years after the work began in 1825, the space being utilised by Birkenhead's first market in the interim. The private gardens were acquired by the council in 1903 and opened up to the public. Since then a statue of Laird, a cenotaph and the Victoria Memorial have all been added. Kellys Directory of 1893 gives an idea of the calibre of resident living there at the time, including twelve physicians, three surgeon dentists, numerous solicitors, a couple of architects and a vicar. Most entries do not include an occupation, however, which indicates that these residents were rich enough not to have to work at all.

Hilbre Island

It is difficult to imagine on a hot summer's day when streams of walkers and picnickers are gathered around Hilbre Island, but this was once a spot so isolated that it had its own monk's cell with a resident anchorite. No one lives on the island now, but in past times it has had its own mill, beacon, lifeboat station, telegraph station, chapel and inn, a haven for drinkers who like a good stay-behind. It even had its own factory in the late seventeenth century processing rock salt. It has been inhabited in one way or another for centuries: Stone and Bronze Age artifacts have been found, along with the ubiquitous Roman pottery – those Romans must have been very careless with their crockery. The island got its name from one Hildburgh, when a chapel was set up for her on the island. Benedictine monks took over the chapel around 1080 and two monks were allowed to stay on after the Dissolution of the Monasteries to operate a shipping beacon.

The island is cut off from the mainland four hours out of every twelve and a thorough study of the tide tables is highly recommended before setting off. The only safe route is from West Kirby via the two smaller islands of the archipelago, namely Little Eye and Middle Eye and takes an average walker one hour. There is no safe route from Red Rocks in Hoylake. In 1586 William Camden wrote in his book *Britannia*, a survey of the islands of Great Britain and Ireland: 'In the utmost brinke of this promonterie lieth a small, hungrie, barren and sandie isle called Il-bre which had sometime a little cell of monkes upon it.'

Hooton Hall and Aerodrome

The area around Hooton is best known by Wirralians as a place they pass through briefly on the way from the M53 towards the Welsh Road, or for the station they pass through on the way to Chester. Lesser known is the fact that it was once known for a large mansion and an airport. The mansion dated back to the seventeenth century and was a Georgian house with seven bays below a hipped roof with pediment. A huge orangery was added to the south and a magnificent clock tower to the north. In 1875 the Manchester Ship Canal was built to the east of Hooton Park, cutting off the hall from the Mersey, and the owner, Richard Naylor, a keen sailor, from his beloved yacht, causing him in a fit of pique to abandon Hooton Hall and move to his Nottinghamshire pile. The hall subsequently fell into a ruinous state and was demolished in 1932, the same year as nearby Bromborough Hall. Like Dawpool, columns were salvaged by uber-scavenger Clough Williams Ellis and made their way to Portmeirion.

The considerable grounds of Hooton Hall were partly utilised to construct one of the very first aerodromes in the country. The hangars constructed here are now listed buildings and were used during the First World War to house American aircraft imported into Birkenhead for the war effort in 1917. These were used to train American

Hooton Hall in 1905.

and Canadian pilots for combat over the Western Front. The military retained use of the airport until 1957 when most of the land was sold for the construction of the huge Vauxhall car plant. The eastern range of the old south hangars are currently used to store a collection of old commercial vehicles, mainly buses.

Hovercraft

There are some inventions that completely transform society: the internal combustion engine, the internet, real ale, cake. Then there are those that burst onto the scene promising much but never quite delivering: the Sinclair C5, gull-winged Delorean cars, Betamax videos, Jedward. The hovercraft falls into the latter category. Wirral has the dubious honour of having the first regular, but short-lived hovercraft service in the world. The main problem, apart from the fact that it was forever breaking down, was the sheer noise out of it. A regular service was mooted in 1961 and a suitable site was sought. Potential routes considered were in the Bristol Channel, the Thames Estuary, the Humber, and the Wash, but the Dee Estuary was the only one to fulfil all the criteria, viz. a firm beach at both ends, high levels of summer traffic, a reasonable distance between termini and separation from shipping lanes.

The original route was to be from Hoylake to Rhyl, but the locals objected so much to the noise that Leasowe was chosen as an alternative – far enough away from any built-up area not to cause a nuisance, but accessed by decent roads. The inaugural flight on 20 July 1962 ended up 100 yards away from the jetty with the twenty-four passengers having to wade ashore, the soggy pioneers having paid £1 for the privilege, and over the next couple

THE WORLD'S FIRST HOVERCOACH

THE VICKERS VA-3 OPERATED BY BRITISH UNITED AIRWAYS ON B P FUELS AND OILS

Postcard commemorating the first commercial hovercraft flight.

of months it only managed to operate on nineteen days of the fifty-nine-day season. The weather had to be perfect for the flight; the British weather being what it is, they had clearly not thought this thing through. The hapless craft was laid up for the winter at Rhyl but was smashed about in the winter storms and never flew the route in anger again. The hovercraft was subsequently moved to the US where it had better luck (and better weather).

I

Irvine, Andrew

One of six children, Andrew 'Sandy' Irvine was born in Park Road South in Birkenhead, in a large three-storey house that would later become the well-known ESWA Sports and Social Club, ably run by Colin and Karen Muir for many years. Raised in a well-to-do and well-connected family, he attended Birkenhead School and Shrewsbury School before he went on to Oxford University. A keen rower, he helped the Oxford team win the Boat Race in 1923, before joining the University Mountaineering Club. His famous climbing companion George Mallory had lived in Slatey Road before joining up with Irvine for their attempt at the summit of Mount Everest in 1924.

It is one of the greatest mysteries of mountaineering whether the intrepid pair actually reached the summit nearly thirty years before Hillary, but following the clues it does appear likely. They were both spotted by team leader Noel Odell 'going strong for the top' high up on the north-east ridge some 100 yards from the summit at 12:50 on the night of 8 June, so it seems inconceivable that they would have failed when so close to their goal. Also, Mallory had promised his wife he would place a photograph of her on the summit and when his body was finally found in 1999, in a state of excellent preservation due to the cold, no such photo was found. Irvine's ice axe and oxygen

George Mallory and
Sandy Irvine at Everest
Base Camp.

cylinder have been found, but the mountain has yet to give up his remains. If he is ever found, his camera may be found with him and perhaps this intriguing mystery will finally be solved.

In recognition of the two brave mountaineers, roads were named after them off Borough Road in Birkenhead, along with one named Everest Road.

J

Jackson, Glenda

This remarkable actress is the only British-born performer to win two Academy Awards. Born into a working-class family in Birkenhead, she started acting when she was at West Kirby County Grammar School, performing for the Townswomen's Guild Drama Group no less. She joined RADA in 1954, making her stage debut in Terence Rattigan's *Separate Tables*. Her first film role was a bit part in the Richard Harris vehicle *This Sporting Life*, a gritty tale of northern folk, rugby league and whippets. She also joined the Royal Shakespeare Company in 1964 before achieving her first Oscar success in 1969 for her performance in D. H. Lawrence's *Women in Love*. TV work was also important to her, appearing as Elizabeth I in *Elizabeth R*, a role for which she had her head shaved. The apogee of her career on the small screen, however, was in a play what Ernie Wise wrote for the *Morecambe and Wise Show*. She played Cleopatra with such timeless lines as: 'All men are fools and what makes them so is having beauty like what I have got.'

Her second Oscar came in 1973 with *A Touch of Class*, a novel achievement for a female British actor. In 1992, however, she gave up acting to further her political career, becoming Labour MP for Hampstead and Highgate in 1992. After disagreements within the Blair government, she again returned to acting, which she continues to this day. She had a theatre named after her in Birkenhead, which was part of the Met College in Borough Road, a site that the Beatles performed in in 1963, although not in the Glenda Jackson Theatre.

King's Gap

Apart from the Battle of Brunanburgh, Wirral has been largely bypassed by the mainstream of English history. One major event has left a small imprint on the peninsula, however. King's Gap in Hoylake is where the massed armies of William III gathered in 1689 and 1690 en route to Ireland and the game of thrones known as the Williamite War. James II had been deposed in the Glorious Revolution and had fled to Ireland where he planned to raise an army and win back the crown. To counter this William sent his most trusted officer, Marshal Stromberg, to Ireland with an army of 10,000 men, embarking from the foreshores of Hoylake and Meols, at the time a major embarkation point and deeper than the current channel through to Liverpool.

The marshal was not up to the job, however, so in 1690 William organised another army and took control himself. His army again mustered at Hoylake and the king joined his troops soon afterwards after stopping overnight at nearby Gayton Hall.

The King's Gap at Hoylake.

While at Gayton he found time to plant two trees called William and Mary and knighted his host, William Glegg. William III strode down to the beach at the spot now called King's Gap, doing a meet and greet with some of the fetid but enthusiastic locals, shaking hands and curing the king's evil as he went. The culmination of his adventures in Ireland was the infamous Battle of the Boyne on 1 July 1690, still fondly remembered by Protestants and reviled by the Catholics.

Lady Lever Art Gallery

Built in 1922 as a memorial to Lady Leverhulme, the wife of industrialist, philanthropist and creator of Port Sunlight Lord Leverhulme, the Lady Lever Art Gallery is the jewel in the crown of the village. Created within the more formal section of the site by William and Segar Owen, it is not the most magnificent of edifices, built in a rather staid neoclassical style. What makes it so special, however, is what lies within. A collection of fine sculptures, Chinese ceramics and the greatest collection of Wedgwood pottery in the world is just a taster for the heart of the collection, the magnificent display of pictures by the leading British artists of the eighteenth and nineteenth centuries. *The Cottage at East Bergholt* by John Constable, portraits by Joshua Reynolds, another by George Stubbs (a horse, of course) and an early work by Richard Wilson, known as the father of English landscape painting.

The Lady Lever Art Gallery at Port Sunlight.

All this, however, is a mere preamble for the remarkable collection of Pre-Raphaelite works accumulated by Leverhulme. Every one of the major Pre-Raphaelite painters are here: William Holman Hunt (*The Scapegoat, May Morning*), John Everett Millais (*A Dream of the Past, Spring*), Dante Gabriel Rosetti (*The Blessed Damozel*), Ford Madox Brown (*Windermere, Cromwell on his Farm*), Edward Burne Jones (*The Beguiling of Merlin*) along with works by the lesser-known, perhaps, but equally talented Frederic Leighton and William Waterhouse.

There are other major works by foreign artists, including Queen Victoria's favourite artist Franz Winterhalter (*Prince Albert*) and John Singer Sargent from the USA (*On His Holidays*). There is also a portrait of Lever himself, painted by Augustus John.

Lees Tapestry Works

This company must surely be one of the most underrated concerns ever to establish themselves on Wirral. At one time they dominated the world market in tapestries and upmarket furnishings, with their products finding their way into the homes of royalty, government and countless industrial and commercial companies. For much of their life they were the only factory in the world producing hand-embroidered tapestries on a commercial basis. The founder, Arthur H. Lee, came from a third-generation textile family; his father founded the famous Tootal brand. Having been cut from the same cloth so to speak, he started a mill in Warrington producing superior quality

Overhead view of Lees Tapestry Works.

textiles, before moving to Birkenhead in 1908 on account of his wife's health, setting up the factory in Stanley Road.

He was joined by his three sons at this time who helped bring in innovations such as their own dye house to speed up the process and add a greater range of colours to the tapestries. They were also forerunners in workers' welfare, introducing pension plans for the workforce well before this became commonplace. During the Second World War they went began producing basic cloths for the military, but after the war demand for high-end wall hangings and tapestries reduced as the whole world became captivated by the new craze for minimalism and bad art.

Lees closed in December 1970 and the factory complex was demolished. Two small supermarkets have now taken part of the large site, with an area to the south taken by a small cul de sac named Tapestry Gardens. The company, however, continues in America under the name of Lee Jofa, the firm having put down roots here as far back as 1903 when they opened an office in New York.

Lighthouses

There are eight extant lighthouses on the Wirral, nine if you include the modern confection of no historic interest built near Red Rocks. In 1761 an Act of Parliament granted Liverpool Trustees powers to construct four lighthouses on the northern coast of the peninsula: two in Hoylake to guide vessels into the deepwater mooring of Hoyle Lake, where ships took shelter in bad weather when they could not make it into Liverpool, and two further east for ships wishing to navigate through the Horse and Rock channels into Liverpool.

The Hoylake lights consisted of a lower light at high-water mark and an upper light further inland in what is now Valentia Road. The two lights were used in conjunction to triangulate a path into the lake. The lower light of 1764 was built of timber and lasted rather remarkably for 100 years before it was replaced by one in brick. It last shone in July 1908 and has been subsequently demolished. The upper light of 1764 was built of brick, but this too was replaced in 1865 by an octagonal structure that survives to this day, lurking incongruously in an ordinary urban garden.

The upper and lower lights further east were built on the Leasowe foreshore in 1763, but when the lower light was washed away in a storm in 1769 it was decided to make the remaining Leasowe lighthouse the lower light, and the upper light relocated over on Bidston Hill. This became the most inland lighthouse in the world, some 1 ¼ miles from the sea. These lights were essential to shipping making the hazardous journey through the narrow Rock Channel into Liverpool and were only extinguished when improved navigational aids made them redundant.

The best known and most prominent lighthouse is, of course, the 90-foot-tall Perch Rock at New Brighton. Now a Grade II* listed building, it was constructed in 1830 and contained a light and three bells – used as a fog warning when required.

The lower lighthouse, Valencia Road, Hoylake.

Strangely, it is the only surviving lighthouse located in the sea. The remaining three lighthouses are all on a smaller scale: there is a 10-foot one installed on Hilbre Island; one at Ellesmere Port, which was built to indicate the location of the lock gates on the Manchester Ship Canal; and a squat little thing at Woodside Ferry, 23 feet tall and looking more like a chess piece than a functional aid to navigation.

The lighthouse at Bidston Hill.

M

Magazines, The

The area to the south of Vale Park in Wallasey, known to this day as The Magazines, still retains a sense of old-fashioned community. Although surrounded by later developments, the nucleus of the village still contains a couple of old pubs, a cobbled road down to the promenade, sandstone walls, one with built-in steps, small cottages, a strange conical building known as the Round House, and the rather incongruous-looking entrance to the Magazine itself. This solid, brooding structure gave the area its name and played a large part in the history of the village. The area was once so remote and inhospitable that it was described as 'a waste of sandhills' – the ultimate put-down. This very remoteness, however, was a positive benefit for the use the authorities had in mind. When vessels arrived in the Mersey they had a legal obligation to remove whatever gunpowder they had on board before being allowed to berth in the river. At the time this entailed moving the powder onto the shore and having it transported by cart through town and up Brownlow Hill to the Liverpool powder magazine – not an ideal scenario.

Common sense finally prevailed, and an area was allocated on the Cheshire side where this hazardous work could take place. Although the first sheds were incredibly

The Magazines
from a 1930s
postcard.

flimsy and clearly not up to the job, more robust casemates were soon built, separated from each other by piles of earth, thick walls and surrounding plantation, all encased in an outer wall, parts of which survive today. Although on average there were 700–800 tons stored here at any one time, no accidents ever occurred, the only explosion being on the *Charlotte*, but this happened after the powder had been returned to the vessel – a spark had ignited loose powder on the deck and the resultant explosion unfortunately killed all but one of the crew. The magazine was eventually moved further upstream, and houses built within the compound, with the mayor and mayoress of Wallasey occupying one of the six houses constructed.

Gateway to the Magazines with the Round House beyond.

N

Ness Gardens

The story of Ness Gardens is usually condensed into a potted history of Arthur Kilpen Bulley who bought the land now known as Ness Gardens, and of his generous daughter Lois who signed it over to the University of Liverpool in 1948. None of this would have been possible, however, without the assistance of the extrovert adventurer George Forrest, Bulley's go-to guy for plants and seeds, who risked life and limb on his many trips to Yunnan in China to bring back hundreds of rare and unique specimens of dried flowers and thousands of seeds. On his first expedition to China he was nearly killed by the local lamas, who did not take kindly to visiting Europeans and their strange ways. In this period of history lamas were not as friendly as the perpetually smirking Dalai Lama would have us believe. Undaunted with this brush with death, Forrest made a total of seven trips and made himself fairly rich and famous, many plants now bearing the *genera forrestii*. The sheer variety and rarity of his finds helped Bulley create the firm of Bees Seeds, which is still going strong today. Many of his other finds still thrive at Ness Gardens; particularly successful were the many varieties of rhododendron he brought back with him.

Other highlights at Ness include the fabulous rock garden, the display of azaleas and the herbaceous borders. Bulley's original 30 acres have now expanded to 64 acres. The setting overlooking the River Dee is one of the finest in the UK, and has been classed as Grade II in the National Register of Historic Parks and Gardens.

New Brighton Football Club

Always in the shadow of their more illustrious neighbours across the river, New Brighton Football Club failed to attract much in the way of records, their only claim to fame being when they had to substitute their usual goalkeeper for the assistant manager in a League game when he was fifty-one years and 120 days old, the oldest goalie ever to play in the Football League and a record that is highly unlikely ever to be broken. Founded in 1921, they were elected to the Football League in 1923 when the Third Division North expanded to twenty-two clubs. They played at Sandheys Park in Rake Lane until 1942 when the ground was destroyed by bombing and this is where they took their nickname of the Rakers, a name immortalised on a cigarette card issued by Ogdens of Liverpool. There is rare footage of the Rakers at Sandheys Park playing Corinthians FC in 1928 on an old Pathé News film now available on YouTube.

They moved to the Tower Athletic Ground after 1942 and remained there for the rest of their existence. They played twenty-one seasons in the Third Division North, narrowly missing out on promotion on goal difference to Nelson in the 1924/25 season. They managed to get to the fourth round of the FA Cup on four occasions, one as a non-League side, but languished in the League until 1951 when they were voted out, being replaced by Workington FC. They soldiered on until 1983 before folding. One player of note was Kenny Campbell, who also played for Liverpool, Stoke City, Leicester City and Partick Thistle, as well as having eight appearances for Scotland. Many older residents will remember the sports shop he ran in Liscard. Other players of note, if only for their archetypal footy names, were Walter Wadsworth, Harry Topping, Wilf Denwood and Billy Fogg.

New Brighton Tower

As James Atherton stood and surveyed the windswept expanse of the north Wirral coast from his vantage point across the water in Liverpool, his mind may well have been swirling with grandiose ideas for this inhospitable place, of fine Italianate villas rising up the slopes each with an unobstructed view of the Mersey, music floating softly over leafy parks from ornate bandstands, the screams of joy from children playing on the golden sands beneath the sturdy iron pier. That all this came to pass is testament to the business acumen of Atherton and his backers, who were possessed of a typically Victorian can-do spirit borne of Methodist values and mercantile fervour. The greatest of the countless attractions to grace New Brighton, however, was surely the famous tower – some 621 feet above sea level and much larger than its trifling rival at Blackpool.

It was a relative newcomer to the New Brighton landscape, however, as it was not constructed until 1897, on rising land to the south of the pier. A great many attractions were based at the foot of the tower including the peerless ballroom, waxworks and a zoo, all set in the Tower Grounds Amusement Park. It was gone by 1921, however. A lack of maintenance during the First World War had rendered it unsafe, so down it came. The fine red-brick building it stood on survived until 1969 when a huge fire completely destroyed it, leaving the resort to struggle on through a slow and painful decline, which has only just begun to be addressed in the twenty-first century.

Tower and Lake, New Brighton

The tower viewed from the ornamental lake in 1902.

The tower from the beach in 1900.

O

O'Grady, Paul

Born in Tranmere in 1955 not far from his favourite bijou tavern, The Seadog, Paul O'Grady began his working life as a social worker in London, spending his spare time dressing up as the Blonde Bombsite Lily Savage and entertaining the great unwashed in the local pubs and clubs. His fame spread and he began his TV work, still as Ms Savage, with *Lily Savage's Blankety Blank*, *The Lily Savage Show* and *Lily Live*. After deciding to try his luck as himself, his success continued with *The Paul O'Grady Show* in ITV, before moving to Channel 4 with *The New Paul O'Grady Show*, which eventually changed back to *The Paul O'Grady Show*. The production team must have spent many hours and numerous meetings before coming up with these snappy titles. They must have torn their artistic souls asunder, however, to come up with *Paul O'Grady Live* for his TV chat show. His TV work now largely revolves around dogs, and he has achieved further success with his radio show, *Paul O'Grady*.

He has received dozens of awards, including a BAFTA and an MBE and he is an Honorary Fellow of John Moores University, but has not rested on his laurels as he has also found time to write his autobiography. In three separate volumes, his first offering *At My Mothers Knee and Other Low Joints* (not Paul O'Grady: The Book) topped the *Times* bestseller list for several weeks. His later two volumes *The Devil Rides Out* and *Still Standing* have also reached the bestseller list. He shows no signs of slowing down either, so we do not expect 'Paul O'Grady, the Retirement Show' any time soon.

Owen, Wilfred

Probably the greatest of all the war poets, Wilfred Owen was born in Oswestry in 1893 but moved to Birkenhead when his father took a job as stationmaster at the nearby Woodside station. There is a blue plaque on a house in Elm Grove, which was one of several homes they took in Tranmere. He began writing poetry well before the First World War, one of his primary influences being the Romantic poets, especially the work of John Keats. It is for his powerful repudiation of war and all its vile workings that he is principally remembered, however. Owen wrote his powerful poem 'Dulce et decorum est' as a denunciation of Roman poet Horace – 'Dulce et decorum est, pro patria mori' (It is sweet and fitting to die for one's country). War, he states, is gruesome, miserable, tragic, awful, not glamorous or worthy. He enlisted on 21 October 1915, but after suffering the trauma of the trenches for over a year he was returned to Britain to be treated for what was then known as shell shock, better-known today as post-traumatic stress disorder or PTSD. He was sent to Craiglockhart Hospital in Edinburgh where he wrote 'The Next War' a chillingly prescient piece. While recuperating, he met that other great war poet Siegfried Sassoon, whom he hero-worshiped, noting to his mother that he was 'not worthy to light his [Sassoon's] pipe'. Sassoon begged him not to return to France, even threatening to shoot him in the leg to prevent him from going.

He returned to active service, however, in July 1918 and was killed in action on 4 November 1918, just one week before the end of hostilities. With added poignancy, his mother received the telegram informing her of her son's death on Armistice Day when all the church bells were ringing out in celebration. There is a memorial window to Wilfred Owen at Birkenhead Library, bearing the legend 'My Subject is War And the Pity of War'.

What passing-bells for these who die as cattle?
Only the monstrous anger of the guns.
Only the stuttering rifles rapid rattle,
Can patter out their hasty orisons*.

Wilfred Owen,
'Anthem For Doomed Youth' (1917)

---

* prayers

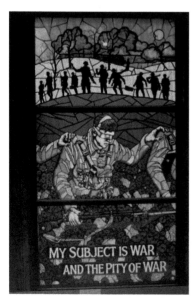

Memorial to Owen in stained glass, Birkenhead Library.

P

Parkgate

An al fresco ice-cream emporium on the west coast of the Wirral Peninsula, on the banks of the River Dee in Cheshire. Named after the deer hunting park established by the Normans and enclosed in 1250, Parkgate was an important port from the start of the eighteenth century. As the River Dee silted up the port of Chester, embarkation points were established further downstream – initially at Burton, then Neston and finally Parkgate – in a futile attempt to outrun the inexorable growth of the silt. Parkgate gradually succumbed as well, accelerated by the deliberate planting of spartina grass on the North Wales side of the Dee at Connah's Quay in 1928 in an attempt to stabilise the intertidal substrata. Before then, however, it was designated as an embarkation point for the important trade route to Dublin from where George Frederic Handel returned in triumph after his first performance of *The Messiah*. Another famous visitor was Emma, Lady Hamilton, sometime mistress to Lord Nelson, who took the waters here in a vain attempt to cure her of a virulent skin condition. It is not known if the good admiral knew of this particular ague or if it would have been of any concern to him. Keen-eyed visitors may have noticed the words 'Nelson' tricked out in black pebbles on a doorstep in Station Road, but these are not related to the admiral.

Mostyn House
School on
the Parade at
Parkgate.

Parkgate Parade in the early 1900s.

Before the quay became unusable local fishermen made a good living out of shrimps, cockles and other seafood caught in the river, a treat still obtainable to this day. Many fishermen also concerned themselves in the far more profitable business of smuggling. So rife was this activity in the area that the authorities set up their own customs house on the foreshore and a lookout post in the old Watch Tower, which can still be seen – it is that building that sticks out on the Parade, causing all the traffic to slow down. On rare occasions the waters of the Dee still lap against the Parade during particularly high tides, attracting an influx of seabirds and twitchers.

Peel, John

Without doubt the greatest DJ that has ever put on a pair of headphones, and he was born in Wirral. Born John Ravenscroft in Heswall on 30 August 1939, he developed a love for music at a very early age, listening to the likes of Radio Luxemburg and the American Forces Network. After moving to America in 1960, Peel started his radio career with a local station and rode the wave of popularity for all things British when the Beatles made it big over there in 1964, moving to a major station in Dallas. After returning to Britain in 1967 he found work with the offshore pirate station Radio London, a job he loved as he could play psychedelic and prog rock as much as he liked. The BBC and the authorities finally closed the pirates down and most of the DJs moved onshore – many to the BBC. Peel became the longest-serving member of this exclusive group, racking up thirty-seven years with the Beeb.

His radio show became extremely popular, in large part because of the appeal of the legendary Peel Sessions, which began in 1967. Between September and December of that year he had Pink Floyd, Traffic, T Rex, Fleetwood Mac, Family, Ten Years After, Hendrix and Bowie in the studio. One of the stand-out policies from the start was in recording unconventional music. An early example of this is when he invited Syd Barratt to perform in February 1970. He always seemed to be ahead of the curve with music trends and there is no greater example than his rapid embrace of the new punk sound emerging from 1977. As ever, though, he mixed things up. Punk bands The Damned, The Ruts and Crass were alternated with Reggae, new wave and post-punk. Even Peter Hammill appeared at the Maida Vale studios. There were over 4,000 Peel Sessions by 2,000 artists, with the record number of appearances by The Fall with their prickly front man Mark E. Smith doing thirty-two.

And then there was the Festive Fifty. Starting in 1976, it listed the top fifty songs of the year as voted for by the listeners and makes interesting reading. In 1976 the top three acts were Led Zeppelin, Derek and the Dominoes and Dylan. By 1979 it was the Sex Pistols, The Undertones and Joy Division. Although he professed never to have a favourite band, Misty in Roots, The Fall and The Undertones must have been up there. To quote John Peel regarding his simple philosophy on music: 'I just want to hear something I haven't heard before.' His death has left a massive hole that has never been filled.

Piers

Due to the nature of the two rivers on either side of the Wirral Peninsula, it was only on the eastern shoreline that piers were created, following the line of the River Mersey. Starting from the south, after passing the promontory of Stanlow, containing the remains of Stanlow Abbey, a scheduled monument with little left to see, the river narrows as it heads past the line of the Manchester Ship Canal and its large dock gates at Eastham. The Eastham Ferry pier appears as a small spur, but it was once a large pleasure pier serving travellers from Liverpool and beyond who flocked to the attractions that once abounded here. Now a pleasant country park, it once housed a bear pit, rides and a monumental entrance arch. Just downstream from here but fairly inaccessible is Jobs Ferry, a purely commercial pier established as early as 1300. Stone steps and some scattered stones are all that remain of this venture.

Passing what was once the hustle and bustle of Bromborough Docks, the portal for raw materials into and finished goods out of the Port Sunlight Factory of Lever Brothers, it is now a backwater next to Prices Bromborough Pool Village. The next pier is at New Ferry, again little more than a stump now but once a busy ferry pier over to Liverpool. Rock Ferry pier has the remains of a wooden pier, which is rapidly falling into the river but has a certain eerie majesty about it. Its near neighbour is now

Egremont Pier in the 1900s.

New Ferry pier in 1903.

the ugly but functional Tranmere Oil Terminal. There was an old pier just south of the Lairds complex called Tranmere pier, but nothing survives, similarly the remains of Monks Ferry comprise a stone groin and a muddle of masonry lying forlornly in the mud to the south. This incidentally had nothing to do with the monks at Birkenhead Priory.

Woodside Ferry pier then looms into view, still a working ferry but less of a transport hub than previously. North again and the site of the old Wallasey pier, which served the Wallasey Dock but has been replaced by the pier for the Stena Line ships. The other working pier remaining is at Seacombe Ferry, which once helped take the strain off the New Brighton pier in the summer season when millions of passengers descended on the resort. Egremont Ferry is now another stump, but at one time was the longest pier on the Mersey. This just leaves the sad tale of New Brighton pier, or rather piers, as one was constructed for travellers to and from the resort, while the other was an entertainment pier with its own theatre and bandstand. Closed in 1972 and demolished five years later, the pier would have proved a massive asset when New Brighton began its renaissance at the beginning of this century.

Port Sunlight

William Hesketh Lever, latterly Viscount Leverhulme, was the driving force behind the creation of one of the finest model villages of the nineteenth century. After making a great success of his soap-making business in Lancashire, he was looking for a new site to expand. Luckily for Wirralians he found it in 56 acres of poor quality, low-lying (but cheap) marshy ground on the banks of the Mersey and with the help of his architect friend William Owen set about creating the marvellous village we see

The bridge over the Dell at Port Sunlight.

today. A total of 24 acres were set aside for a factory to produce his wildly popular Sunlight soap. The remaining 32 acres were used to create high-quality housing for his workforce. A special dock was also created from the river to the factory to facilitate the movement of raw materials in and finished products out.

Lever's benevolent despotism necessitated the construction of a series of buildings for the care and well-being of his workforce, the first being Gladstone Hall off Greendale Road in 1891, just three years into the project, opened by William Gladstone himself. The Lyceum in Bridge Street came next, quickly followed by Hesketh Hall, Hulme Hall and that most valuable of resources, the pub. The Bridge Inn was originally a teetotal establishment as Lever scorned the drinking of alcohol, but to his credit he agreed to it becoming a proper inn when the workforce started kicking off about it. Despite some losses during the war the village remains largely as Lever left it – a delightful sylvan oasis amid the urban sprawl.

Hesketh Hall, Port Sunlight.

Quarries

Visitors to Wirral often mention the extent of sandstone walls in the area, all of which have been taken from the dozens of local quarries that once dotted the peninsula. Most people are aware of the largest one: Storeton Quarry on Mount Road in Bebington, which is now a popular recreation area. There are many clues left of its presence, even if it is difficult to appreciate its sheer scale today. Remnants of the old tramway that brought stone from the quarry to Bebington quayside can still be sought out, including the old tramway tunnel that ran under Mount Road and where 200 workmen were invited to a grand dinner when the tramway was completed, although this is now filled with the detritus of years of neglect. The old gatekeeper's cottage can still be seen on the west side of Cross Lane with an extant

Grannys Rock at the Breck Quarry.

pair of sandstone gates further south that lead into Quarry Avenue – another clue. There was an equally deep but smaller quarry on the east side of Mount Road, but very little remains of this.

Luckily, a few abandoned quarries have been made into open recreation grounds for the public to enjoy. The nearby Arno is one of the finest; another popular location is the old Irby quarry in Royden Park, but the one with the finest views, across the north Wirral Plain, is the Breck in Wallasey. The huge workings at Queen Street where the Holborn Square Industrial Estate now lies contain bricked-up caves where the people of Birkenhead sought shelter during the bombing raids of the last war. Other abandoned quarries are harder to seek out, with perhaps just a sheer wall remaining. Holt Hill quarry, Flaybrick quarry on Tollemache Road and the quarry at Strouds Corner in Wallasey fall into this category. The walls of the large Lingdale quarry can still be made out at the backs of houses in Brancote Road Birkenhead. No trace remains of quarries located in Quarry Lane Heswall, Westway Birkenhead, the Tower Grounds New Brighton and doubtless many more.

Queen Victoria Memorial

On the demise of Queen Victoria in 1901 after nearly sixty-four years on the throne, many towns across the country sought to construct lasting memorials to their sulky sovereign, Birkenhead among them. The Victoria Memorial Committee was duly formed and an attempt was made to raise enough money by public subscription to erect a bronze effigy to the queen. The great unwashed, however, were not as forthcoming with their hard-earned cash as the committee had hoped. Perhaps rather too many had remembered Victoria's ceaseless mourning over the loss of her husband Prince Albert – obsessive morbidity is never a good look. They therefore plumped for Plan B, a cheaper granite and sandstone monument in the shape of an Eleanor Cross, a nod to Edward I who had visited the town during his reign. The original Eleanor Crosses had been built at each resting place where Eleanor of Castille's coffin lay overnight on her final journey down to Westminster Abbey. The cost of the cross was £1,400 and was designed by Edmund Kirby, who refused a fee for his work.

Placed in the centre of Hamilton Square at the meeting point of four diagonal paths, the 75-foot-high memorial is impressive, possibly more so than the original bronze effigy would have been. It takes the form of an octagonal shaft, rising in stages to a crocketed spire with a crown finial above. A decorated frieze at the base contains the arms of Birkenhead, Chester, Wales, Ireland, Scotland, England and the royal arms, together with the rather strangely worded legend 'Victoria, Queen and Empress. She wrought her people lasting good.' Known as the 'Wedding Cake', it was granted Grade II status by English Heritage in 1974.

The memorial at the centre of Hamilton Square.

RAF West Kirby

There were two RAF bases located on Wirral at one time. RAF Hooton was the larger base, with an airstrip and hangars, and full training facilities for pilots and ground crew. RAF West Kirby on the other hand was designed to accommodate the lowest rank of personnel, the AC2s. Opened in 1940, some 150,000 men had received basic training at West Kirby before its closure in 1960, most as part of their call up to national service after the war, between 1949 and 1960. They were housed in basic wooden barracks, twenty men to a hut, laid out on the site in four nearly identical zones, each with a parade ground, cookhouse and NAAFI store.

The most basic of training regimes were undertaken such as the obligatory square bashing, rifles (naming of parts), and a little history of the RAF thrown in. After eight weeks they were assigned to other camps throughout the country for more rigorous education and training. Although named after the nearby West Kirby, the actual station was located in Larton, some 3 miles away, just south of Saughall Massie Road. No record remains of its existence as the camp was turned back into farmland. The only physical reminder is a memorial located nearly opposite Oldfield Road, consisting of a large stone on a flat base with an attached upended plane propellor and a plaque commemorating those who trained and worked here. Although there was no airfield here, trainees were taught the basics and, judging by the very active website dedicated to the base, it is remembered with fondness by many.

Railways

The development of the railways within Wirral was Machiavellian and is best left to experts in the field. The basics are, however, that a railway was needed from Chester to Liverpool and the quickest route was through Wirral, via Woodside. The tunnel under the Mersey through to James Street in Liverpool was opened in 1886 – the first rail tunnel

Old railway cutting on the line to Seacombe.

below a river anywhere in the world. Lines were extended to New Brighton and West Kirby, which are now under the Merseyrail banner. A little-used line still runs down the centre of the peninsula, from Bidston to North Wales. Known as the Borderlands Line, it is operated by Transport for Wales. There are now just three stations within Wirral, namely Upton, Heswall Hills and Neston, and trains only run once an hour. The third line of note was closed to passengers in 1956; it was the western route from West Kirby Joint station to Hooton, which is now the Wirral Way (see page 88). Of greater interest than the existing stations is, however, tracking down evidence of closed stations on the line. Monks Ferry station in Birkenhead branched off the main line to a jetty on the banks of the Mersey where coal was transported to waiting barges.

A sandstone bridge parapet survives in Church Street along with a nearby stretch of wall nearby. More remains of the former Town station in Waterloo Place where the bridge into the station crossed the road here, and there is also evidence in adjacent Jackson Street. The Luke Street bridge parapet over the Seacombe branch line remains at the far end of the supermarket car park on Church Road, but the main evidence remaining is the large cutting made for the line, which is now the approach Road for the Wallasey Tunnel. One further survivor can be found at Burton Point station on the North Wales line where the yellow-brick station house remains as part of Station House Nurseries.

Bridge to old Town Station, Waterloo Place, Birkenhead.

River Dee

The two rivers marking the eastern and western borders of the Wirral Peninsula could not be more different. The River Dee is wide, shallow and slow-moving as it passes the peninsula, forming a wide estuary as it flows out into Liverpool Bay. At 113 kilometres long, it rises in Snowdonia at Dduallt (black hill), flows down through North Wales past Llangollen and into Cheshire, past Chester and the old Dee bridge before being canalised west of Chester and widening out on the border of Wirral. It is difficult to imagine the historic importance of the river for trade, but it was once a major trading route to and from Chester and Ireland, Germany, and Spain.

The Romans named their major fortress after the river and it retained its importance until gradual silting forced the embarkation points further and further downstream, with Shotwick, Burton, Neston, Parkgate, Dawpool and Hoylake all having their moment in the sun as the major port on the Dee before the silt arrived. Industry has mainly been concentrated on the Welsh side with steel production, chemicals, paper production and a large power station. The only major contributor on the Wirral side was the colliery at Ness, which stretched under the Dee for several miles at one time.

The River Dee looking downstream from Parkgate.

The River Dee looking upstream from Parkgate.

The estuary now caters for more leisurely activities as well as being home to some 100,000 birds who nest in the marshlands here. The Dee Estuary is now a Site of Special Scientific Interest, a Special Protected Area, a Special Marine Area and has large areas designated as a nature reserve by the Royal Society for the Protection of Birds.

River Mersey

Rising near the viaduct in Stockport, the River Mersey takes a meandering route west before joining the Manchester Ship Canal near to Carrington Power Station. It then sneaks out again by Woodston Nature Reserve before continuing its rambling journey towards Runcorn where it widens out considerably between Hale on the north bank and Weston Point on the Cheshire side, reaching its widest point of 3 miles across between Eastham and Liverpool Airport. Narrowing again to just over 1 mile across between Woodside and the Pier Head, it again widens as it flows out into Liverpool Bay.

The Mersey here led, of course, to the massive growth of Liverpool from the seventeenth century, with the massive dock system from Herculaneum Dock in the south to Seaforth Dock in the north, stretching some 7 miles. From a Wirralian's point of view, however, the river was more of a barrier to growth rather than a highway. It was linked to Liverpool by ferries, but these were slow, unreliable and downright dangerous in rough weather. It was not until the first tunnel was dug in 1886 for the Wirral Railway that the Wirral began to benefit from the trade generated on the Lancashire side, and tradesmen from Liverpool began to settle on the quieter Wirral Peninsula. Wallasey, Birkenhead and Bebington all became dormitory towns for Liverpool.

Traffic increased further with the opening of the two road tunnels: Queensway in 1934 and Kingsway in 1971. In the meantime, access improved on the ferries with safer and

The River Mersey from Eastham Ferry.

The River Mersey from Magazine Promenade.

more reliable vessels plying between Woodside, Seacombe and Liverpool for workers during the week, with Egremont and New Brighton ferries catering for the holiday crowds in the summer months. The view from Wirral across the Mersey has always been full of interest but several landmarks have been lost, notably what was known as the Three Sisters, a series of chimneys at Clarence Dock Power Station that came down in 1994.

Rock Park

Rock Park consisted of over fifty large Victorian villas and was one of the earliest residential park developments in the United Kingdom. The introduction of a steam ferry service in 1830 had stimulated development of the area and a group of Liverpool merchants, all keen to escape the noise and grime of the city, formed a joint stock company in 1836 with the snappy title of the Rock Ferry Company. They drew up plans outlining the required size and location of building plots, to be serviced by a serpentine road and two lodges manned by wardens to keep out the hoi polloi. The design of the properties was to be left to individual landowners subject to various quality criteria. The result was an upper/middle-class enclave of superior sandstone villas, many with fine views back across the Mersey to Liverpool.

Rock Park was complete by 1850 and attracted many local worthies to the area, most famous of whom was Nathaniel Hawthorne, the American consul to Liverpool, who resided at No. 26. He clearly loved the place as he remarked, 'Never were there such noiseless streets, a police station at the entrance has an officer on duty, allowing no

Above: Rock Park with a view across to Liverpool.

Left: Rock Park at its finest.

ragged or ill-looking person to pass.' A later tenant of No. 26 was an astronomer by the name of Isaac Roberts, who installed a 2-foot telescope in a specially designed revolving dome in the top storey, which was unfortunately destroyed in an air raid. What survived the war was ruthlessly sliced in half in the 1970s when the New Ferry Bypass was cut through the estate. This municipal act of wanton vandalism has completely spoilt the integrity of one of the finest examples of Victorian estate planning. Fortunately a few areas remain to remind us of what has been lost at the altar of the motor vehicle.

S

Scouts Jamboree

To celebrate the twenty-first anniversary of the inaugural meeting of the Boy Scout movement in Birkenhead in 1908, organisers felt it appropriate to hold its Jamboree in Birkenhead. Arrowe Park was chosen as the venue due to its vast size – it's the largest park in the United Kingdom. Even so, it was still not large enough to accommodate the 50,000 scouts from all over the world that attended, and overflow sites were set up in Overchurch and Woodchurch. The Jamboree was opened by the Duke of Connaught, the proceedings commencing with a huge inaugural march past.

The feeding of the 50,000 was quite an operation, with so many different diets and religions it was a culinary nightmare. The volumes consumed were mind-boggling: 42,000 tins of sardines, 17 hundredweight of marmalade, 5 tons of tea, 22 tons of water biscuits, 50,000 loaves, 10 tons of onions, 1,200 gallons of milk... the list goes on. Each country had its own allotted camp area where they could host scouts from other countries; the French contingent even built a model Eiffel Tower in their zone from scout staves. The largest tent on site was, of course, for Baden-Powell, whose tent was nicknamed the Ritz. There was a cinema, a market and a daily paper called *The Daily Arrowe*.

The only thing the organisers did not have a hold on was the weather. It poured down incessantly for most of the fortnight, turning the park into a mud bath, especially after some 320,000 visitors paying 1s each had walked across the site. No one was too disheartened, however, and everyone had an unforgettable time. One amazingly overgenerous side issue was the ruse to get every Scout in the world to donate 1d to the movement, the proceeds going to buy the chief Scout a Rolls-Royce, a cheque for £2,000 and a portrait of himself. I do wonder if my humble efforts in Bob-a-Job week in the 1960s contributed to the cost of a gold-plated Lamborghini and a fat cheque for some bloated pooh-bah with a woggle.

Seacombe Pottery

John Goodwin was a master potter from the epicentre of the pottery industry: Stoke on Trent. He had set up is Crown Pottery Works to produce superb quality ceramics

Seacombe Pottery by Harry Hopps (*c.* 1900).

primarily for the domestic market. His sons meanwhile had moved to Canada, and it was this market that Goodwin turned to when he moved his factory and most of his workforce to Seacombe in 1852, ensuring that he would be nearer Liverpool Docks and the lucrative export trade to the colonies and provinces. His distinctive premises consisting of six dome-shaped kilns and associated workshops were located in Wheatland Lane and survived until 1906.

His two sons expanded the business in Canada, with his son George opening a large factory in Toronto. They introduced a range of plates with views of London, marked with the Seacombe brand, which command prices above £1,000 each at auction today. The popularity of his ironstone range of kitchenware such as soup tureens, bowls, platters and plates made a move across to Liverpool necessary, and the short-lived Seacombe factory closed in 1864. His sons continued the business after John Goodwin's death, but disaster struck in 1870 when a large consignment heading for America was lost at sea. The goods were not insured and the company was dissolved soon afterwards, unable to suffer the loss. Amazingly, a dish was recovered off the coast of Puerto Rico in the 1990s bearing the name of the Seacombe Pottery and it is believed to be part of the lost consignment.

Submerged Forest

It sounds like something from Jurassic Park, but this feature off the coast of Meols to the north of the peninsula still occasionally puts in an appearance when the tides contrive to force the sands to shift. The last time this happened was in 1982 when substantial areas of the peat bed emerged from the bay. There was a large area exposed around Leasowe in the 1920s, and up until the 1950s the beds were visible for several miles – a large amount of material was collected for analysis at this time. With improvements in technology such as carbon dating it has been shown that pine trees dating back to 2300 BC and oak trees from around 2500 BC were present.

The coast extended for several miles further than the current position, but rising water levels following the last Ice Age killed the trees and swallowed up vast tracts of land. Villages were said to have been drowned by the rising waters and in the nineteenth century a large horde of gold, jewellery and more mundane items such as knives and spoons were discovered, indicating a substantial community existed here. Accounts from the sixteenth and seventeenth centuries relate how large trunks and branches were still exposed at this time, with the local population making good use of this resource, taking the wood away to make furniture and ornaments. Even part of the library at nearby Leasowe Castle was made of wood from the submerged forest. During reconstruction of sea defences in 1978 examples of strata exposed during the works were found to contain ox ribs and antlers from boars and red deer.

The Submerged Forest at Meols in 1903.

Thornton Manor

One of the best-known mansions in Wirral. Located just outside Thornton Hough village, this Grade II* listed building is more famous for its illustrious owner, William Hesketh Lever, later to become Viscount Leverhulme, who lived at the property between 1888 and 1919, retaining ownership until his death in 1925. The house was initially bought to house Lever's expanding collection of furniture and *objets d'art* that he had accumulated over the years, and was one of the principal reasons for expanding the property in 1896, a job undertaken by architects Douglas and Fordham, who had done much work for Lever in Port Sunlight village. Among the many valuable pieces were paintings by John Everett Millais and Frederic Leighton, two of the leading lights in the Pre-Raphaelite movement so favoured by Leverhulme.

The grand entrance lodge to Thornton Manor.

Thornton Manor from the west.

No Victorian mansion would have been complete without a conservatory, and Lever's at Thornton Manor was one of the largest, elements of which survive today. Ferns were a bit of an obsession with the Victorians, but Lever brought in many other rare species that were too delicate to survive in the unpredictable English climate. The grounds at the manor were extensive, covering 50 hectares and included paths, a summer house, a dell and a large lake. Situated to the west of the house, the picturesque lake is now used as a backdrop for weddings and other large functions.

The manor has played host to many famous people, including heads of state and prime ministers, most notably our own dear Boris who held private talks on Brexit here with Irish Taoiseach Leo Varadkar. The Queen Mother was a regular visitor, being a good friend of the Third Viscount; they shared a common interest in horses and horse racing. On the death of the viscount the house was sold, the contents making a record £10 million at auction in 2001.

Training Ships

For over a century the view across the Mersey from Rock Ferry to Liverpool was broken by the bulky silhouettes of several sailing ships, looming up like spectres in the morning haze, the *Akbar* especially earning this eerie reputation. Anchored offshore from the early 1830s, it began its life on the Mersey as a quarantine ship for cases of bubonic plague, cholera, typhus and smallpox before becoming a juvenile reformatory training ship for Protestant boys of age eleven to fifteen. Life on board was incredibly brutal, with punishments such as the cane and birching commonplace. Accidents were frequent and often fatal, and in winter the boys suffered from pneumonia, tuberculosis and asthma. This dreadful regime eventually came ashore and changed its name to the Heswall Reform School, but the beatings continued, even Winston Churchill, no stranger to a damn good thrashing when at Harrow, thought it appropriate to launch an inquiry into the school but nothing was ever done.

The *Clarence*, also moored off Rock Ferry, was a reformatory ship for Catholic children, being classed as sinful was an added burden for the damaged children on board this particular vessel. The *Akbar* and *Clarence* were the equivalent of floating sink estates compared with the *Indefatigable* and the *Conway*. The Indefatigable was a fifty-gun frigate loaned by the Admiralty for use as a training ship for the sons and orphans of sailors, and kitted out as such through the generosity of James Bibby of the famous shipping family who donated £5,000 to this end. The first boys came aboard in 1865 and the vessel was used until 1912 when it was replaced by HMS *Phaeton*, sold by the Admiralty, and fitted out at the expense of Frank Bibby and renamed *Indefatigable* again, having the figurehead of William IV swapped over from the old ship to the new.

HMS *Conway* was a cadet school ship for the training of officers for the mercantile marine and it appears that they did a good job in turning out well-rounded and confident individuals if the list of former alumni is anything to go by. Captain Webb, the first man to swim the English Channel, Buster Crabbe, the famous diver who

Training ships *Conway*, *Akbar* and *Indefatigable*.

disappeared in mysterious circumstances when spying for the Admiralty underneath a Russian battleship, Poet Laureate John Masefield, rugby legend Clive Woodward and Tory politician Iain Duncan Smith were all old boys. The *Conway* was moved to Menai Strait during the Second World War but ran aground on the way back to the Mersey and was wrecked, eventually being set alight. So ended the interesting but tumultuous history of the training ships of the Mersey.

Trams

George Francis Train moved from America to Liverpool because of his shipping interests in the White Diamond Line, but it is not for ships that he is remembered. Acting as an agent for Robert Morris, a Philadelphia banker who had financed street railways in the States, Train set about convincing the Burghers of Birkenhead that a tram on rails was a far better idea than a tram on cobbled streets. The advantages were obvious: horses can pull greater loads on rails, the ride is far smoother and once the initial costs of infrastructure had been absorbed it was likely to make a tidy profit. Unfortunately, many of the wealthier citizens objected as the tracks were to be laid at the side of the road, making it difficult for gentlemen to access their private carriages. Cab drivers also thought, rightly so, that it would impact their business. The idea, however, was too good to pass up and the tracks were laid from 1860, the first street railway in Britain, initially from Woodside to Birkenhead Park but gradually

Wallasey tram en route to New Brighton, 1902.

expanding to the well populated areas around Oxton and Claughton villages. Cabmen continued to protest, deliberately getting in the way of the trams and slowing them down to a crawl. This did not go down well with passengers, however, and there was a report in the *Daily Post* in December 1861 of tram passengers attacking cabmen with frozen lumps of snow, with one unfortunate fellow being thrashed with his own horse whip. The horse trams continued in the town and to a lesser extent in Wallasey until electrification took over in around 1900. The trams ran in Wallasey until 1933, with Birkenhead following suit in 1937 when diesel propulsion took over. Trolleybuses were envisaged and a deputation went to Wolverhampton for a demo, but they were never adopted.

Tranmere Rovers

Formed in Birkenhead as Belmont FC, Tranmere Rovers changed to their current name a year later. In 1887 they moved their ground to Temple Road when the ground was renamed Prenton Park, a name they retained when a further move to their current location was made in 1912. The pitch in Temple Road was located at the bottom end where it meets Borough Road, the land subsequently being used for the construction of Devonshire Park School and Parkhurst Road. They became founder members of the Third Division (North) in 1921 where they remained until 1961 when they were relegated to the 4th Division. Regular promotion and relegation followed

The Tranmere Rovers First Eleven, 1910.

during the 1960s and 1970s with the nadir being reached in 1987 when the club went into administration. Enter Johnnie King. Under his tutelage Tranmere Rovers won promotion to the Third Division in 1989 and the Second Division in 1991, winning the Associate Members Cup on the way. They were involved in three play-off campaigns, reaching the final against Notts County – those of us who were unlucky enough to watch Rovers lose 2-0 also had the chirpy warblings of Chesney Hawkes at half time to contend with. The Super White Army were back at Wembley in 2000 for the League Cup Final, which they lost to Leicester City 2-1 and after this highlight they eventually dropped out of the Football League before reclaiming their place three years later. Rovers most famous player was undoubtably Dixie Dean (see page 23), but there have been other famous players, many coming from the two bigger Merseyside clubs, including Ron Yeats, Tommy Lawrence, John Aldridge, Ronnie Moore, Bunny Bell, Pongo Waring, Steve Coppell and Pat Nevin.

U

Upton Manor

William Inman was born on 6 April 1825 in Leicester, moving to Liverpool when his various business interests expanded. Most famous for the Inman Shipping Line, his increasing wealth brought a move away from the noisome atmosphere of the city in 1854, over to the more pleasant surroundings of Wirral. He purchased Upton Hall, a large villa in the centre of the village where he stayed for three years. He found the vicinity so appealing that he persuaded his parents, two brothers and his sister to move over to Wirral where they settled in the Spital and Rock Ferry areas. While at Upton Hall he commissioned architect John Cunningham to build him a grand

Upton Manor.

mansion to the north of Upton. Harefield House, as it was originally known, named after the family seat in Harrogate, was built between 1857 and 1860 within 300 acres of parkland – the site once encompassed all the land between Ravenstone Close and Manorside Close. When Inman purchased the lordship of the manor of Upton in 1865 he renamed it Upton Manor and had the large belvedere tower constructed so that he could view the comings and goings of his ships on the Mersey, a fleet that had grown to eighteen ships and carryied 44,000 passengers a year. As with most businessmen of his ilk, he used his wealth for the benefit of the community, providing funds for the construction of churches in Upton and Moreton. On his death it was bought by another shipowner, Ralph Watts. It has had various owners and periods when it lay empty, eventually being bought by the Faithful Companions of Jesus, who already occupied Upton Hall. It was used as a junior school by the FCJ sisters from 1950, but was sold in 1987 and is now a nursing home. The story of Upton Manor serves as a template for many of the grand mansions built in the nineteenth century in the north-east corner of Wirral.

Vikings

'From the fury of the Northmen O Lord deliver us.' Any Wirralian bearing an old Wirral name that can be traced back at least 300 years has more than a 50 per cent chance of having Norse DNA. This is living proof that the Vikings were not just horn-headed pillagers but often came to settle in the lands they had invaded. The Norse raiders did not come directly from Scandinavia, but via Ireland – a quick row across the Irish Sea. Plenty of evidence for their occupation was already available before the genetic trail study was undertaken, of course. Physical evidence such as coins, pins, broaches and weapons have been found in abundance, especially along the Meols shoreline; even evidence of a complete Viking longboat has been detected under the car park in front of the Railway Inn at Meols.

The Railway Inn, home to a Viking longboat.

Fragments of Viking crosses have been found on Hilbre Island and in the basement of St Mary's and St Helen's Church in Neston, a preaching cross in Bromborough and a complete hogback grave cover discovered in West Kirby made of a grey sandstone not found locally. The final major clues as to their presence here comes in the profusion of Norse place names throughout the peninsula. The suffix 'by' is Norse for settlement, so we have Raby (border settlement), Frankby (Frank's settlement) and Greasby (wooded settlement). Tranmere translates as cranebird sandbank and Meols as sandbank. Thingwall is where they held their parliaments, being the Norse word for assembly. One final Viking exclusive for Wirral lies in the fact that this is the only place in mainland Britain with documentary evidence of Norwegian Viking settlers, with one Ingimund being mentioned on the surviving document.

Water Towers

Along with church steeples, spires, windmills and beacons, water towers create marvellous landmarks across the vistas of Wirral. Built for purely practical reasons, it exemplifies the psyche of the Victorians that they built such beauty into functional architecture. What would be constructed today as a soulless steel drum was crafted into castellated towers, Norman keeps and soaring Gothic piles – a legacy that we should cherish. Water towers were built on high ground, of course, for practical reasons, the water being fed to consumers via gravity. This made areas such as Oxton and Heswall practicable for urban expansion in the nineteenth century. The Heswall tower has unfortunately gone. It once stood on the highest point on Wirral, but only the names of Tower Road North and Tower Road South are left to remind us of its existence.

The Flaybrick Hill water tower.

Gorsehill water tower at New Brighton.

The Oxton area was served by the Flaybrick tower, which still stands proud on Boundary Road, 50 feet high, complete with tank and attendant reservoir. It was built by the Birkenhead Improvement Commissioners between 1862 and 1865 and is now a private residence. Just visible from here is the New Brighton water tower, 82 feet high, octagonal, castellated, machicolated and with an attached stair turret, a marvellous piece of work created by the Wallasey Corporation in 1863. 9 feet higher, but in a less-prominent spot is the brooding mass of the Mill Lane tower, built in a Norman style by the Local Board of Health in 1861, this monster was capable of holding 150,000 gallons. One other water tower remains, different from those mentioned in so many ways. Located in Quarry Road Hinderton and now a private residence, this small private water tower was created by Alfred Waterhouse no less, designer of Manchester Town Hall and the Natural History Museum in Kensington, and built in 1884 by Christopher Bushell to pump well water into his home, Hinderton Hall, with surplus being sent down to Neston village. Such generosity and community spirit earned him a nice fountain, given by grateful villagers in recognition of his largesse, it still stands at the crossroads in the centre of the village. A large water tower supplying Prenton has been dismantled although a large reservoir remains.

Wirral Way

Following the original line of the old London & North West and Great Western Joint Railway, the Wirral Way was Britain's very first linear park. It is not just a fine walk, it retains much railway paraphernalia and infrastructure, from gradient posts, random sleepers, bridges and cuttings to whole platforms and a complete station preserved in aspic for the casual tourist and railway buff alike. Opened in 1866, the railway originally ran from Hooton to Parkgate, extending to West Kirby some twenty years later. It was a single line with passing points along the route and was utilised by farmers moving produce to market and coal from the nearby Ness colliery, which had its own branch line near Parkgate Road at its Neston end.

A mile out of Hooton station there was a small branch line that led up to Royal Ordnance Factory No. 10 from 1942 until the end of the war. Next came the first station on the branch line: Hadlow Road. In the 1930s there were three porters at Hadlow Road station all with the surname of Davies. Their first names were Tom, Dick and Harry. The station has been marvellously preserved with its original ticket office, old advertising and a relaid length of track. An old signal box purloined from Cheshire completes the ensemble. An angled level crossing gate heads west towards a deep rock cutting and Neston station – no trace of this remains. Turning north, the line passed Parkgate and Heswall stations before reaching Thurstaston station where an entire platform survives, before travelling on through Caldy and Kirby Park and on to its final destination of West Kirby Joint station, sited where the current Concourse now sits.

The preserved station at Hadlow Road.

Deep cutting at Neston on the Wirral Way.

Unfortunately, there are a couple of stretches where the builders moved in before the whole line could be preserved, but a quick walk along a tarmacked road and you are soon back in the 1950s. The Wirral Way proves what can be achieved with a little imagination and is a valuable asset for all Wirralians.

Woodside

The area around Woodside was Birkenhead's main transport hub for many years, a position it has now lost due to a decline in the use of public transport. The Victorian railway station at Woodside was one of the greatest examples of railway architecture in Britain. Built in 1878, lines ran out in a great arc from the station into a tunnel beneath Chester Street before emerging at the old Town station and ultimately joining the main line down to Paddington station in London. Two bridges were constructed just south of the station; the one spanning Rose Brae has been demolished, but the one over Church Street survived the demolition of Woodside station in 1969 – another act of municipal vandalism from soulless planners whose insensitive, utilitarian diktats were propagated on the often flawed recommendations of Dr Richard Beeching, that bête noir of every rail enthusiast. A large model of the station can be viewed in the nearby Town Hall, however.

To the south of the station a series of eleven graving docks stretched down the Mersey, all belonging to Grayson Rollo ship repairers. A small jetty can still be made out, which is what remains of Monks Ferry, the original disembarkation point for pilgrims in the care of the monks from the nearby Birkenhead Priory. This area south of the station was blighted by the overpowering stench of an abattoir, a glue factory and a tannery – a situation many Birkonians will recall with fondness.

Tramlines and buses at Woodside Terminal.

The Ferry Boat at Woodside, with Albert Dock beyond.

X-craft and Submarines

Although no X-craft were built at Lairds during the Second World War, their expertise was used by the makers Vickers Armstrong of Barrow to construct these potent mini-submarines, which were used for special operations throughout all theatres. They were also used for reconnaissance operations off the coast of Normandy in preparation for D-Day in 1944. Cammell Lairds did, however, build many larger submarines for use in the war effort. The most prominent submarine built in the shipyard, HMS *Thetis*, became famous for all the wrong reasons when she sank during sea trials in Liverpool Bay in June 1939. An inner hatch in one of the torpedo tubes had been opened while an outer hatch was also open, allowing sea water to enter the vessel. Only four men managed to escape before the escape chamber was jammed. The rest of the ninety-nine men on board perished. The boat was eventually salvaged and repaired, entering service as HMS *Thunderbolt*, but this in turn was lost with all hands when it was attacked with depth charges off the coast of Sicily, which is where this wretched ill-fated craft remains.

Lairds built sixty-nine submarines between 1915 and 1992 and now contribute to the Astute hunter-killer submarines for the navy on a modular basis. A model of

The model of *Resurgam* at Woodside Ferry.

the world's first mechanically powered submarine can be seen at Woodside Ferry in front of the ferry terminal. *Resurgam II* was built by J. T. Cochran, a Birkenhead shipbuilder, in 1879 (*Resurgam I* was a 9-foot prototype) and was 45 feet long, 10 feet in diameter and weighed 30 tons with a crew of three brave souls. After trials in the East Float, it headed for Portsmouth for a demo in front of the Royal Navy top brass but never made it, sinking off Rhyl in February 1880, fortunately without loss of life. The wreck was miraculously found in 1995 by an experienced wreck diver, but attempts to raise her have to date proved fruitless. One final submarine of note, of course, is the *U534*, displayed at Woodside since 2009. Built in 1942, she was used as a training boat for the Kriegsmarine so was not involved in the sinking of any Allied vessels. She was attacked and sunk by the RAF three days before the end of hostilities in Europe and salvaged in 1993.

German U-boat 534 on display at Woodside.

Y

YMCA

The Young Men's Christian Association was founded in 1844, with active branches throughout Wirral from an early date. They played a major role in the war effort between 1914 and 1918, setting up their Bebington headquarters on land now occupied by the Oval Sports Centre, where soldiers on leave from the trenches received accommodation, food, entertainment, prayers and readings. It is from here that the local Bantam Regiment was formed – Bantam being men deemed too small for inclusion in regular units of the army. The Birkenhead Grange Road headquarters was built in 1890 at a cost of £9,000, having moved from smaller premises in

The original YMCA building in Grange Road.

Conway Street. The Grange Road building still stands, although the ground floor is now a branch of Primark. It was here that the Boy Scout movement was officially inaugurated by Lieutenant General Baden-Powell on 24 January 1908.

His idea for a Scout movement had been born out of his experiences in the Boer War and he felt that the movement could grow more rapidly through associations with organisations such as the YMCA, a 'possible growth point' as he put it. His book *Scouting for Boys* coincided with the launch in Birkenhead, and the rest, as they say, is history. Many troops, including the First Birkenhead, claim to be the first Scout troop in the country, but there are stronger claims for troops in Sunderland and Glasgow.

If this historic event was not enough, the Grange Road YMCA also claims to be the original home to basketball in the United Kingdom. President of the YMCA in Birkenhead at the time, C. J. Proctor, started the first basketball league in the country at Grange Road, having watched the game in Canada. The league widened into a Wirral League with other early interest being shown in Birmingham and elsewhere. Having spawned two major organisations, the YMCA moved to their Whetstone Lane premises in 1935 due to financial problems, it was here that the Beatles played in September 1962 before performing another show at the nearby Majestic Ballroom later in the day.

Z

Zeebrugge Raid

The raid on the port of Bruges-Zeebrugge on 23 April 1918 was an attempt by the Admiralty to block the port and prevent German U-boats based there from leaving. There was an existential threat to Allied control of the English Channel due to the marauding U-boats, thus justifying this most perilous of plans. The idea was to block the harbour entrance by scuttling obsolete ships, with an obsolescent cruiser, HMS *Vindictive*, and the Mersey Ferry boats *Daffodil* and *Iris II* creating a diversionary attack on the mile-long mole covered by a smokescreen. Unfortunately for the British forces, the wind direction changed and the smokescreen blew offshore, enabling the defending Germans to turn their fire on the three exposed vessels. All three were badly damaged despite being covered in armour plating, and had to limp home after great loss of life. Some damage was caused to the port and it was blocked for a couple of days, but U-boat attacks resumed soon afterwards.

Damage to the bridge of HMS *Iris* during the Zeebrugge Raid.

The whole escapade was deemed a heroic failure, but it was never through lack of bravery, with no fewer than eight Victoria Crosses being awarded – several posthumously. The two ferry boats had been requisitioned by the Admiralty because of their shallow draughts, which enabled them to pass over mines unscathed, with watertight compartments making them virtually unsinkable (had they not learned from the *Titanic*?). They returned to a hero's welcome in the Mersey, resuming their ferry duties in 1919 with the prefixes 'Royal' in recognition of their contribution. Although the raid proved unsuccessful, valuable lessons were learned, which were put to good use in the next conflict.

Damage to the main deck on the *Iris*.